North Carolina
Wildflowers

A children's field guide to the state's most common flowers

Interpreting the Great Outdoors

Text by Beverly Magley, Illustrations by DD Dowden

For Matthew and Emily,
with love
from Aunt Bevy

Copyright © 1993 by Falcon Press Publishing Co., Inc.,
Billings and Helena, Montana.

Botanical consultant: Rob Sutter, Southeast Director of Biological Conservation,
The Nature Conservancy, Chapel Hill, North Carolina.

On the front cover: spring beauty, violet, cardinal flower, dogwood, and
dogtooth violet.

Design, editing, typesetting, and other prepress work by Falcon Press,
Helena, Montana. Printed in Singapore.

Library of Congress Number 92-055082
ISBN 1-56044-184-4

Contents

Introduction

Wildflowers can be fragile or as tough as nails. They can grow on the highest mountain or underwater in a swamp, along a busy footpath or beside the salty sea. They can endure weather that sends people running for cover and then lift their cheerful blossoms to the sun the very next day.

Flowering plants have existed for about 120 million years. They evolved when dinosaurs roamed the earth. They are unique because each of their seeds has a protective, nourishing shell that helps the seed survive. And survival is the primary goal of every living thing.

Wildflowers entice visitors with their nectar, and the nectar-eaters then pollinate the blossoms so they can produce seeds. A nice trade! So when you see an ant crawling inside a flower or watch a hummingbird sipping nectar, remember they are essential to the survival of flowers. In addition to providing food, flowers may provide shelter for insects and other little creatures.

North Carolina provides different kinds of homes for wildflowers. The mountains create different living conditions from the plains. The seashore differs from swamps and freshwater streams. Most flowers are adapted to specific conditions, but a few flowering plants are so versatile they can live almost anywhere.

Please don't pick wildflowers. If you pick a flower, it dies. If you leave it blooming in its home, the blossom will eventually scatter seeds that will provide another year of beautiful wildflowers you can come back to enjoy.

Wildflower, when I look on thee
All that's wild and sweet in me
Soars free

Sanna Porte Kiesling

Longleaf Pine Forests—Wet Longleaf Pine Forests

Longleaf pine forests are one of the most threatened habitats in North Carolina. The pines have needles and cones more than a foot long. They grow above open, parklike grasslands that harbor many flowering herbs, including orchids, asters, and insect-eating plants. Fire is necessary to maintain this forest. In fact, all the species are adapted to fire and grow better if a fire occurs every one to six years.

Longleaf pine forests have nearly been eliminated. Many have been replaced by agricultural fields, or the timber industry has planted forests of quicker-growing species.

Longleaf pine forests occur in two types: a wet forest found close to the coast between New Bern and Wilmington and a dry forest that surrounds the town of Southern Pines.

Venus Flytrap

other names: none
height: 4 to 12 inches
season: May to June

This amazing, rare plant exists only in southeastern North Carolina. Spiders and insects are attracted to the color and the nectar inside the leaf. If they move two of the sensitive hairs on each leaf, the leaf snaps shut and traps them inside. The plant slowly digests the bugs and then reopens to await another victim.

Dionaea muscipula

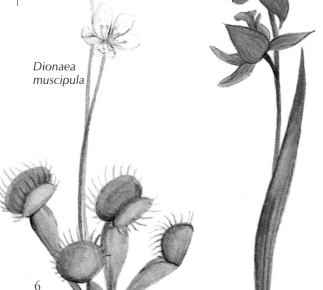

Grass Pink

other names: none
height: 6 to 20 inches
season: March to August

Calapogon comes from the Greek word for "beautiful beard." See the little "mustache" of golden hairs? Lean close to sniff the wonderful fragrance of this exquisite orchid. You'll find just one grasslike leaf on each plant.

Calapogon spp.

Sundew

other names: none
height: 4 to 9 inches
season: June to August

Sundew leaves look like round green suns with little shiny rays. When insects investigate this plant, the leaf hairs fold over and the bugs get stuck in the gooey drops produced by the leaf. The sundew takes several days to suck the nutritious juices from an insect. Then the leaf opens up and the bug skeleton dries up and blows away. Yuck!

Drosera rotundifolia

Pitcher Plant

other names: Trumpets
height: 8 to 24 inches
season: May to August

Sweet nectar on the edge of the pitcher-shaped leaf entices insects. A bug can easily crawl down the tube, but tiny, barbed, downward-pointing hairs on the inside of the leaf prevent it from climbing back out. When the insect falls into the bottom of the "pitcher," plant fluids and bacteria digest the unlucky critter.

Sarracenia purpurea

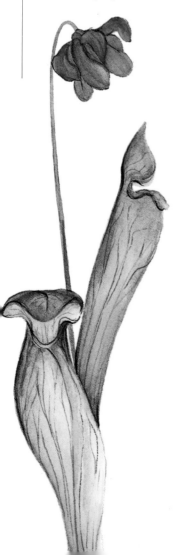

Blazing Star

other names: Snakeroot
height: 2 to 4 feet
season: August to September

In autumn, blue is the most common flower color in longleaf forests. Blazing star blossoms add to this blue haze beneath the pines. The clusters of frilly, purplish-blue blossoms closely packed on the erect stalks brighten dry mountain slopes and ridgetops. The lower leaves are grasslike.

*Liatris
graminifolia*

Ladies' Tresses

other names: none
height: 6 to 24 inches
season: August to October

The twisted, braided flower spikes look like tresses, or long hair. But this orchid was originally called ladies' traces, because it also looks like the laced-up corsets women once wore.

Spiranthes spp.

Prickly Pear

other names: Cactus
height: up to 5 feet high, with clumps 10 feet across
season: April to June

Prickly pear is an abundant and widely distributed cactus. The leaves of cacti have evolved into spines to conserve water and to keep animals from eating the succulent stems, known as pads. The prickly pear's tasty fruit, called a "tuna," is a juicy, burgundy-colored, pear-shaped treat enjoyed by both humans and animals. Be sure to peel off the tiny spines, called glochids, before eating the fruit.

Opuntia compressa

Sand Stinging Nettle

other names: Tread-Softly, Spurge Nettle
height: 6 to 36 inches
season: March to September

Ouch! Don't touch this plant, because the tiny needlelike hairs could poke your skin and inject a stinging juice. The sting goes away after awhile. The root grows very deep into the ground. While this plant isn't used for anything, closely related species provide rubber and tapioca.

Cnidoscolus stimulosus

TRADESCANTIA Spiderwort family

Spiderwort

other names: Widow's Tears, Moses-in-the-Bulrushes, Trinity Flower
height: 8 inches to 2 feet
season: April to June

The arching leaves look like the splayed legs of a spider. Spiderwort's delicate flowers bloom in the morning and turn into a jellylike blob by afternoon. This plant is especially sensitive to radiation and may help warn us about dangerous pollution.

Tradescantia rosea

Compass Plant

other names: none
height: 3 to 6 feet
season: June to September

Perhaps this is called a compass plant because the blossoms face the sun all day, moving from east to west. Pretty sunflower-like flowers perch atop tall, round, stout stems.

Silphium compositum

Lupine

other names: Hairy Lupine
height: 8 to 24 inches
season: April to July

Lupus is Latin for "wolf," and the lupine got its name because early people thought it gobbled nutrients in the soil. But today we know that wolves are a positive part of the natural world, and we've also learned that lupine actually enriches the soil it inhabits.

Lupinus villosus

British Soldiers

other names: Red Crest Lichen
height: .5 to 2 inches
season: year-round

This isn't really a flower, although the red color may catch your eye like a blossom does. British soldiers is a lichen. Lichens are a unique cooperation between algae and fungi. The algae use photosynthesis to convert sunlight to energy, while the fungus uses the energy and provides nutrients the algae need. Lichens can grow on many surfaces, such as wood, rocks, and—here in the dry longleaf pine forests—bare sand.

Cladonia spp.

Piedmont Bottomlands

The bottomland forests of the central part of North Carolina are home to many wildflowers, as well as such trees as oaks, hickories, sugarberries, elms, walnuts, dogwoods, and ironwoods. Some trees measure more than ten feet around!

The soil here is very fertile because nutrients wash in with the annual floods. In springtime, many wildflowers carpet the forest floor even before the tree leaves emerge. You can watch for shy deer, busy beavers, and playful river otters. Later in the summer, the bottomlands teem with insects, especially ticks, so late summer isn't a very good time to hike here.

Dogtooth Violet

other names: Trout Lily,
    Adder's Tongue
height: 6 to 10 inches
season: March to April

Some bottomlands are thick with these nodding yellow flowers. This plant isn't really a violet. It's a lily, as one of its other common names indicates. The "trout" in trout lily comes from the mottled brown splotches on the leaves that look like the freckles on a brown trout. Deer nibble the leaves and green seedpods.

Spring Beauty

other names: Groundnut,
    Fairy Spuds
height: 2 to 10 inches
season: April to July

Look closely to see the thin pink lines and spot of yellow decorating the flower. Each of the five petals is notched at the top. Indians ate the nutty-tasting corm, a thick underground base.

Claytonia virginica

May-Apple

other names: Mandrake
height: 12 to 18 inches
season: April to June

In springtime, a group of May-apples looks like a crowd of parasols. A single white flower blooms below the leaves of large plants. It looks like an apple blossom, and it blooms in May. The roots, leaves, and seeds are poisonous, but you can make the bitter, golden fruits into a flavorful jelly. Turtles and raccoons like to eat the fruit. An ingredient taken from the roots is used to make a medicine that removes warts.

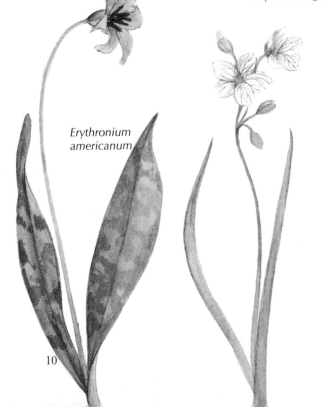

Erythronium americanum

Podophyllum peltatum

Yellow Lady Slipper

other names: Noah's Ark,
Whippoorwill Shoes
height: 4 to 28 inches
season: April to June

A brilliant yellow lip petal forms a tiny ballet slipper complete with long, striped, purple petals ready to tie around a tiny ankle. Bees are good at retrieving the nectar, but other insects get trapped inside by the curled lower lip.

Cypripedium calceolus

Bloodroot

other names: Red Puccoon
height: 6 to 10 inches
season: March to May

The roots and stem of the bloodroot contain a bitter, reddish-brown juice used by Indians to dye baskets and clothing and make war paint and ceremonial decorations. The plant's scientific name *Sanguinaria* comes from the Latin word for "blood." The pure white blossom springs out of a large, curled leaf, opens fully in the sunshine, and then closes each evening.

Sanguinaria canadensis

Jack-in-the-Pulpit

other names: Indian Turnip
height: 1 to 3 feet
season: March to May

Some people think this plant looks like a preacher standing in a fancy, old-fashioned, covered pulpit. The striped spathe forms a little roof to protect the flowering spadix. Gently lift the spathe: The plant is female if the flowers look like tiny green berries. It's male if the flowers have little threadlike stamens and are dropping pollen. Insects fly from plant to plant and spread the pollen. Indians cooked and ate the corm of this plant.

*Arisaema
triphyllum*

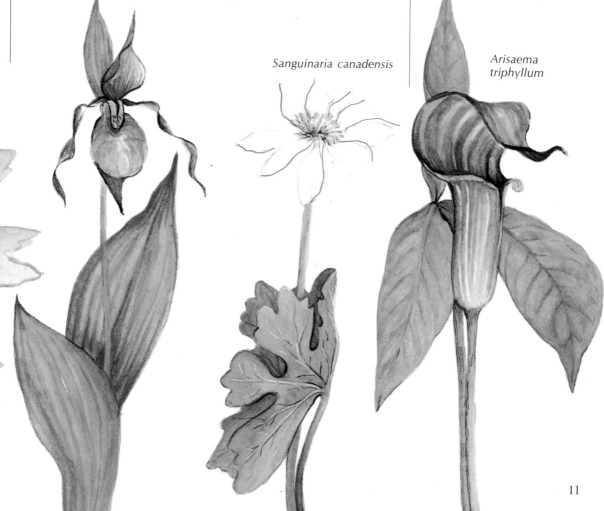

Piedmont Forests

Early settlers were impressed by the forests of central North Carolina. They wrote of riding horses through open woods of towering oaks and hickories. Today, most of the Piedmont forests are gone. The trees were cut for timber and the land turned into farmland or townsites. Most of North Carolina's major cities are located in the Piedmont, close to water and agricultural lands.

Bluets

other names: Quaker Ladies
height: 3 to 6 inches
season: April to June

A golden sunburst brightens the center of each blue blossom. At night, the flower closes tightly and nods as if sleeping. But the next morning, it's wide awake and open, reaching toward the sun. Look for the furry beefly, which sticks its long tongue into the flower tube to suck out the nectar. Another woodland dweller with the name bluet is the damselfly with a metallic-blue abdomen.

Wild Ginger

other names: Snakeroot
height: 6 to 12 inches
season: April to May

You have to be very observant to spot a shy, wild ginger blossom with its long, tapered, petal-like bracts. The leathery, heart-shaped leaves are shiny, and the brownish flower lies close to the ground where it's easy to attract pollinators such as beetles and springtails. Ants love to eat the fatty seeds, so they gather and store ginger seeds underground, helping to disperse them.

Blue Violet

other names: Violet
height: 3 to 8 inches
season: March to June

A small pouch behind the lower petal has little guide lines on the landing platform to direct bees to the nectar. Violets are edible. The leaves have lots of vitamins A and C, and the blossoms are sometimes used to make candy, jelly, and syrup.

Houstonia spp.

Hexastylis spp.

Viola papilionacea

Cranesbill

other names: Sticky Geranium, Wild Geranium
height: 1 to 2 feet
season: April to June

Deer like to eat these flowers and leaves. In late summer, it's easy to see how a geranium got its scientific name. *Geranos* is Greek for "crane," and the fruit looks like the beak of a crane. If a fruit pod is ripe and still closed, touch it gently and watch the tiny cups fling seeds through the air.

Geranium maculatum

Sundrops

other names: Primrose
height: 2 to 4 feet
season: June to September

Each fragile yellow blossom releases a wonderful fragrance as it awaits pollination. The leaves taste peppery, and some people eat the fresh roots in springtime. This plant produces as many as 6,000 seeds, and goldfinches love to gobble them.

Oenothera fruticosa

Passion Flower

other names: Maypop
height: climbing vine
season: June to September

This blossom's common name refers to Easter, which is also known as "The Passion of Christ." Early Spanish explorers thought the flower head and fringed edges represented Christ on the cross with a crown of thorns. The blossom often pops open in May. The edible, lemon-colored, egg-shaped fruit has an odd, sweet flavor.

Passiflora spp.

13

Dogwood

other names: Flowering Dogwood
height: to 30 feet
season: April to May

The beautiful, white, spring blossom of the dogwood tree is North Carolina's state flower. But look closely and you'll see that the flower isn't a flower at all. What look like white petals are actually white leaves surrounding small green flowers. Indians made a scarlet dye from the alligator-skin bark and used it to color feathers, clothing, and blankets. The tough, hard wood is useful for making mallets, golf-club heads, pulleys, weaver's shuttles, thread spools and bobbins, and chisel handles. Squirrels and birds love to eat the shiny red berries in autumn.

Cardinal Flower

other names: Scarlet Lobelia
height: 2 to 4 feet
season: July to September

These blossoms are scarlet like the bright plumage on a cardinal. The color attracts hummingbirds and butterflies that feed on the nectar. Shake some seeds into a bag and take them home to plant in a wet part of your garden.

Redbud

other names: Eastern Redbud,
 Judas Tree
height: to 40 feet
season: March to April

Brilliant magenta-pink blossoms cluster on the redbud tree in early spring— so early that the leaves haven't even dared to unfold yet. Look closely at the flowers or the fruits and you'll see that this plant belongs to the bean family. You can add the blossoms to a salad or fry them like fritters. Yum! Bobwhites and other birds munch on the brown seeds in autumn.

Lobelia cardinalis

Cornus florida

Cercis canadensis

Mountain Bogs and Wetlands

Joe-Pye-Weed

other names: Purple Boneset, Queen
of the Meadow, Trumpet-
Weed, Gravelweed
height: 2 to 6 feet
season: July to September

According to one story, an
Indian named Jopi, or Joe Pye,
taught early settlers to cure
typhoid fever with this
medicinal plant. There are
more than forty species of
Eupatorium, and most of them
have medicinal uses. The most
common species in mountain
wetlands has a thick, hollow
stem with many whorls of
pointed leaves. The reddish-
purple flowers often grow
more than five feet above the
ground.

Most people don't like to climb through areas thick with
rhododendron branches and slog through muck that comes
over their boot tops. But if you do, you may emerge in the
interesting bogs and wetlands of the mountains. Perhaps
you'll find a sunny opening carpeted with sphagnum, with
hummocks of flowering plants. If you're lucky, you'll see a
rare bog turtle.

Most people avoid walking in mountain bogs. But it's
worth the effort. Bogs are the most threatened and the rarest
habitat in the mountains. Many have been destroyed to make
way for highways, agriculture crops, and homes.

Gray's Lily

other names: none
height: 2 to 6 feet
season: June to July

This is a very rare,
threatened lily that grows only
in the southern Appalachians.
Look for its nodding red
flower in bogs and on
mountain balds. Perhaps you'll
see a hummingbird sampling
the sweet nectar.

Beebalm

other names: Mint, Oswego Tea
height: 2 to 5 feet
season: June to August

Tiny, bright red flowers form
clusters around the square
stem. Look closely at the
leaves with a magnifying glass.
The tiny, golden drops of oil
you see give the plant its
strong minty smell. You can
steep the leaves and make a
tasty pot of tea.

Lilium grayi

*Monarda
didyma*

*Eupatorium
fistulosum*

Mountain Forests

Mountain forests contain many different kinds of trees and shrubs. North Carolina has some forest areas that contain more kinds of trees than all of Europe. Some wildflowers live beneath these trees in areas of dense shade and shelter, while other flowers prefer the open forest floor. Streams gurgle, and animals find food and shelter. Black bears still live in some mountain forests.

Many of the birds found here migrate from the tropics to breed in these forests. Look for the flash of scarlet tanagers and listen for the call of the black-throated green warbler, "zee-zee-zee-zu-zee." Listen for the creak of two trees rubbing against each other, and watch for squirrels dashing up and down trees.

Mountain Laurel

other names: Calico Bush, Spoon Wood, Broad-Leaved Laurel
height: 4 to 20 feet
season: April to May

An unmistakable reddish-purple line traces the center of these pink blossoms. Look closely at the flower and you'll see that all the stamens are tucked inside the petals. When a bee lands in the flower, the stamens flip out and cover the bee with pollen, which the insect carries to the next flower. If eaten, the leaves, shoots, and berries are poisonous to people and cattle. Even honey made from this nectar is said to be poisonous. But people have applied the powdered leaves externally to treat skin deseases and rheumatism.

*Kalmia
latifolia*

Fraser's Magnolia

other names: Mountain Magnolia, Umbrella Tree
height: 30 to 70 feet
season: April to May

Close your eyes and inhale the fragrance of the magnolia blossoms. Wonderful! The large leaves on this tree crowd together, and you'll stay fairly dry if you stand under the tree and use it as an umbrella in a rainstorm.

Magnolia fraseri

Showy Orchid

other names: none
height: 5 to 12 inches
season: April to June

The showy orchid has a cluster of white and pink flowers above a group of clasping leaves. There are more than 15,000 kinds of orchids, and they grow nearly every place on earth. Some grow on the bark of tropical trees, while others grow from the ground. The long, dark seedpods of one kind of orchid look like giant string beans and have a delightful, popular flavor you know: vanilla.

*Orchis
spectabilis*

Trillium

other names: Large-Flowered
   Trillium
height: 8 to 18 inches
season: April to June

"Tri" in the name trillium means three: three large green leaves, three white petals that turn pinkish with age, three sepals, three styles, and three reddish berries. One trillium has the common name "wake robin" because it blooms early in the spring—about when the first robins arrive. Some hillsides in the mountains are covered with hundreds of trilliums. But the plant dies quickly if picked.

Trillium grandiflorum

Rhododendron

other names: Rosebay, Great
   Laurel
height: to 20 feet
season: June to July

The scientific name comes from the Greek word for "large rose-tree," referring to the exquisite blossoms that cover this shrub each summer. The leaves are evergreen. Many people plant rhododendrons in their yards. When growing in the wild, these plants can form dense thickets impossible to walk through.

Rhododendron maximum

Solomon's Seal

other names: Smooth Solomon's
   Seal
height: 8 inches to 3 feet
season: May to June

The scar left when the stalk breaks away from the rhizome is thought to look like the official seal of King Solomon of olden days. Maybe so—and maybe not. But the plant's scientific name describes it well: *Polygonatum* means "many knees" and refers to the little swellings at each leaf node. Indians taught early settlers to eat the starchy rhizomes. The dangling flowers become hard green berries that turn dark blue in fall.

*Polygonatum
biflorum*

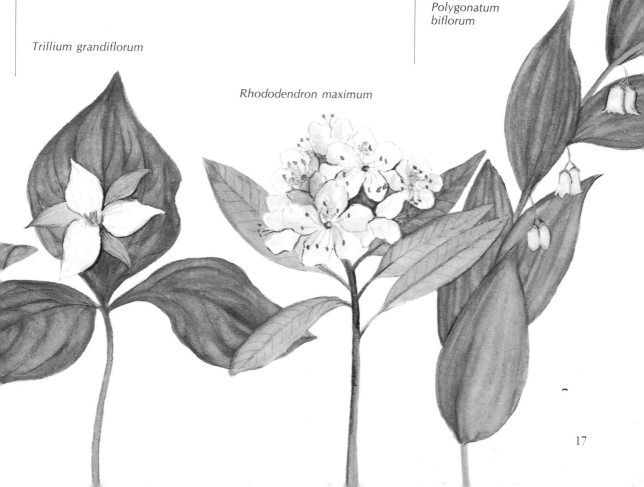

Partridgeberry

other names: Checkerberry, Winter
    Cloves, Deerberry, One-Berry
height: 4- to 12-inch creeping stems
season: June to July

The furry-looking, cream-colored blossoms produce bright red, edible berries. Sometimes you'll find last year's berries among this year's blossoms. Indian women brewed a tea from the leaves to help make childbirth easier.

Columbine

other names: none
height: 1 to 2 feet
season: April to July

Hummingbirds use their long beaks to sample the nectar of columbines, but short, stubby bumblebees must drill holes in the spurs to get at the sweet prize. The name columbine comes from the Latin word *columba*, meaning "dove." Can you see the five doves with their shared wings outspread?

Aquilegia canadensis

Turk's Cap Lily

other names: none
height: 3 to 7 feet
season: July to September

This blossom reminds some people of a Turkish fez, or cap. Some plants may produce as many as forty blossoms! Reddish freckles dot the orange petals, which curve backward so far they nearly touch behind the blossom. Indians dug the bulbs and cooked them in soups.

Lilium superbum

Mitchella repens

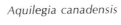
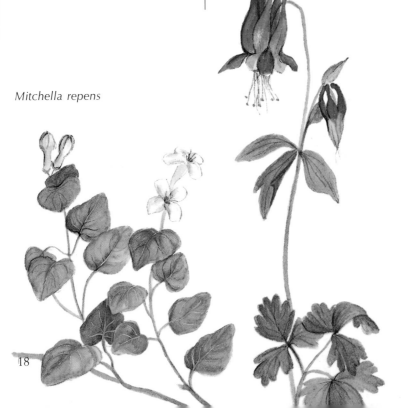

Beard Tongue

other names: Large-Flowered Beard
   Tongue
height: 2 to 4 feet
season: May to June

Such a funny-faced flower! A beard of long yellowish hairs dangles from the lower lip of each tubular blossom, while the upper lip has what look like two tiny teeth projecting forward. Hummingbirds and insects with long mouth parts love to feed on the sweet nectar hidden deep inside the flower.

Penstemon grandiflorus

Indian Paintbrush

other names: Painted Cup
height: 1 to 2 feet
season: May to July

Look carefully for the narrow, pale-green flowers hidden among the bright red, orange, or yellow bracts. The roots of a paintbrush can burrow into the roots of a different plant and steal part of its food. Because of that ability, paintbrush is called a root parasite.

Castilleja coccinea

Jewel Weed

other names: Spotted Touch-Me-
   Not, Snapweed
height: 2 to 5 feet
season: July to October

This flower was named for the sparkling water droplets left on its leaves after a rain or heavy dew. An oil in the leaves causes water to bead up rather than flow off. The same oil is said to relieve the itch of poison ivy and insect bites. Hummingbirds, bees, and butterflies go after the nectar in these peculiar blossoms. Touch a seed capsule gently: if it's ripe it will burst open and scatter the seeds more than three feet through the air.

Impatiens capensis

Spruce-Fir Forests

You'll find spruce-fir forests only on the highest mountains in the state. They're dark, moist, and full of the scent of fir. These forests remind many people of the forests of Canada and New England. Fog is very common, and snow can fall almost any month of the year. But enough sun shines here to ripen the blueberries and provide seeds for the many squirrels, goldfinches, and wrens.

Many of the spruce-fir forests look dead, with whitened trunks covering the peaks. This was caused by rain and fog full of acids generated by power plants and automobiles. These forests are examples of how interconnected our world is. The pollution from cities and industries can affect the forests high in the mountains.

Wood Sorrel

other names: Oxalis, Shamrock
height: 3 to 6 inches
season: June to August

In the dark shade of the spruce-fir forests, the ground may be covered with wood sorrel blossoms. The tiny pink blooms rise above heart-shaped, cloverlike leaves. The leaves have a pleasantly tart taste. The leaves are sensitive to cold and often droop at night.

White Violet

other names: Sweet White Violet
height: 3 to 5 inches
season: May to July

How odd! It seems like a violet should be violet, not white. But the only purplish color on these violets is in the tiny veins and in a hint of color on the back. There are more than 300 species of violets in the world, and they come in many colors.

Bluebead Lily

other names: Yellow Clintonia
height: 6 to 24 inches
season: May to June

Ragged, drooping, shade-loving, greenish-yellow flowers rise above the shiny oblong leaves. The blue beads referred to are actually beautiful blue berries. They're lovely to look at, but don't eat them because they're somewhat poisonous.

Clintonia borealis

Viola pallens

Oxalis montana

Turtlehead

other names: Lyon's Turtlehead
height: 1 to 3 feet
season: July to September

Can you see the shape of a turtle's head in the blossom? Like real turtles, this flower likes moist places. Peek inside the blossom to find a woolly beard of golden hairs on the lower lip. Watch as a bumblebee pushes itself inside the narrow opening. It looks like the "turtle" is swallowing the insect.

Chelone lyonii

Canada Mayflower

other names: Lily of the Valley,
    Two-Leaved Solomon's
    Seal
height: 2 to 6 inches
season: May to June

These tiny blossoms smell wonderful! The bloom time is described by the scientific name *Maianthemum*, which means "May flower." The bright green, heart-shaped leaves collect dew and raindrops that trickle down to water the roots. Clusters of red berries adorn this plant in autumn.

Maianthemum canadensis

Fireweed

other names: Willowherb,
    Blooming Sally
height: 2 to 6 feet
season: July to September

Fireweed is often the first plant to grow after a forest fire. It helps enrich the burned area so that other plants can move back in. The flower blooms from the bottom up, so you may see seedpods, flowers, and buds on one plant. The seeds can be carried long distances by their little parachute-like hairs.

Epilobium angustifolium

21

Beaches and Dunes

The coast is a world of shifting sands, salty ocean spray, and a hot, drying sun. Some plants avoid much of this stress by growing in the sheltered areas behind sand dunes. Others have adapted to shifting sands by growing from underground connections called rhizomes instead of waiting for conditions to be just right for sprouting seeds. Many have roots that extend deep into the ground, both for stability and to find fresh water.

You can look for wildflowers and seashells and build sand castles. Crabs scuttle sideways across the sand; sandpipers race up and back with the breaking waves, and seagulls fish for their meals.

Virginia Creeper

other names: False Grape, Five-Leaf Ivy
height: climbing vine to 30 feet
season: July

The greenish flower clusters are not very showy. In autumn, the leaves—arranged in whorls of five—turn bright red, and tiny bluish-black berries entice birds to come and feast. Virginia creeper climbs on almost anything: fences, houses, trees, boulders, and thickets. It clings tightly with its aerial rootlets and provides nice shade in the heat of summer.

Parthenocissus quinquefolia

Arrowleaf Morning Glory

other names: Railroad Vine, Goat Foot Morning Glory
height: climbing vine
season: June to November

The rolled-up flower buds unfurl into lovely, funnel-shaped blossoms that smell very sweet while blooming. They twist again as they wilt. This flower grows on sand dunes and beaches. Thick, leathery leaves help the plant preserve moisture in its dry, sandy environment. This wildflower is related to the sweet potato.

Sea Purslane

other names: none
height: sprawling vine
season: all year

Purslane grows on the salty ocean shore. Its dark reddish-purple blossoms rise above the juicy leaves. Some people like to eat the young shoots. You can boil sea purslane to get out some of the saltiness.

Ipomoea sagittata

Sesuvium portulacastrum

22

Carolina Jessamine

other names: Yellow Jessamine, Carolina Woodbine, Evening Trumpet Flower, False Jasmine
height: climbing vine to 17 feet
season: January to April

The fragrant yellow blooms herald the coming of spring along the coast of the Carolinas. This is South Carolina's state flower, and it's pictured on the state license plate. In areas protected from salt spray behind the dunes, Carolina jessamine twines over shrubs and up trees. The flowers are poisonous, and some people think the honey made from them tastes bad, too. After flowering is finished, the rootstock has been used medicinally as a calming tonic.

Gelsemium sempervirens

Sea Ox-Eye

other names: none
height: 6 to 20 inches
season: July to September

Yellow blossoms rise above the thick, succulent leaves of this plant. Large colonies of sea ox-eye grow in areas flooded only by the highest tides, between the dry sands behind the dunes and the salt marshes. This plant is so abundant it may cover acres of sand. It spreads and grows from underground rhizomes, which are stems that can store food.

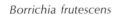

Borrichia frutescens

Blanketflower

other names: Brown-Eyed Susan
height: 8 to 30 inches
season: May to first frost

Blossoms of this bright flower can blanket a field in showy colors. Individually, each flower is like a fiery pinwheel. Look closely at the blossom, called a composite; the brightly colored pinwheel parts are called ray flowers, and the center disk is made up of dozens of tightly packed, individual florets. Look for this one growing behind the dunes.

Gaillardia pulchella

Coastal Wetlands

Pull on your rubber boots to look for these flowers. Plenty of water on the coastal plain has helped to create a unique environment for plants. Many have evolved adaptations that allow them to grow in water, such as spongy stems full of air or leaves that float.

You can find bogs, shallow ponds, lakes, and marshes all along the coast. If you live inland, look in roadside ditches to find many of these same plants. Keep your eyes open for the many frogs that live in the wetlands. They range from bullfrogs the size of your hand to small tree frogs no bigger than a dime. Some of the tree frogs are neon green.

Broad-Leaved Arrowhead

other names: Duck Potato, Wapato, Water Nut
height: 1 to 4 feet
season: July to September

Inconspicuous female flowers hide below the showy male blossoms, awaiting the falling pollen. The leaves are usually shaped like arrowheads, but when the plant grows in a strong water current, the leaves look like long streamers. Ducks and muskrats eat the roots, and Indians taught early settlers to roast the roots.

Sagittaria latifolia

Wild Iris

other names: Blue Flag
height: 2 to 4 feet
season: May to June

Iris was the Greek goddess of the rainbow—and a rainbow of colors appears in the center of these blossoms. In some countries, the three petals symbolize faith, wisdom, and courage. In Europe, an iris was often carved at the top of a queen's or king's scepter. Indians twisted the silky leaf fibers into twine and rope for fishing and hunting.

Iris spp.

Spider Lily

other names: none
height: 20 to 32 inches
season: March to May

Six narrow petals droop around the inner cup like the long legs of a spider. Real spiders have eight legs, though. The bulb may lie dormant for years until conditions are just right. Then this lily sends up its lovely blossom. The scientific name *Hymenocallis* means "beautiful membrane" and refers to this plant's delicate, cuplike flower.

Hymenocallis caroliniana

Cattail

other names: Bulrush
height: 3 to 9 feet
season: May to July

Ever had a cattail pancake? Indians used every part of this plant. The pollen makes a flour for pancakes, breads, or cakes; the leaves can be woven into baskets; the downy seeds are good insulation and make good pillow stuffing or absorbent padding for diapers; and the roots are edible. Many roadside ditches have large stands of cattails with green swordlike leaves and brown sausagelike clusters of flowers.

Typha spp.

Swamp Rose Mallow

other names: none
height: 2 to 5 feet
season: July to September

The gummy juice from the leaves of this plant has been made into cough drops and into an ointment to soften chapped, rough hands. The plant is part of the mallow family, which has many notable members, such as cotton and okra. Next time you toast a marshmallow over a campfire, remember that marshmallows were originally flavored with a European species of mallow.

Hibiscus moscheutos

Atamasco-Lily

other names: Easter Lily, Zephyr Lily
height: 8 to 25 inches
season: April to June

The scientific name *Zephranthes* comes from the Greek story about Zephyr, the west wind. This flower blooms around Easter. It isn't a true lily, an example of how confusing common names can be.

Zephranthes atamasco

Roadsides and Disturbed Areas

People have had a major effect on the plant communities in North Carolina. We bulldoze roads, dig ditches, build railroads, and make trails. We build homes and plant garden flowers that go to seed and sprout elsewhere. Sometimes fires burn an area, or a flooding river rushes through.

Disturbances can alter habitats and restrict many plants to a small portion of their original range. But people have also created new habitat, such as yards, gardens, agricultural fields, roadsides, and roadside ditches.

Various plants have made these new habitats their home. Some of these plants are native species that adapted to some form of disturbance, but many have been introduced from Europe or the tropics. They are all known as weeds.

Weeds have a bad image. They get in your garden and yard and grow where you want tomatoes or grass instead. But weeds are also beneficial. They stabilize soil, decrease erosion, add needed nutrients, and prepare the way for shrubs and trees to grow again. And some weeds can be attractive, such as the butterfly weed and chicory.

Dandelion

other names: Blowball
height: 2 to 12 inches
season: year-round

The word dandelion comes from the French words *dent de lion*, which mean "teeth of the lion." Look for the five little teeth at the outside edge of each yellow floret, and at the jagged, toothlike leaves. The leaves, roots, and flowers are edible and contain calcium and vitamins. Some people remove warts by putting the milky juice from the stem on them.

Partridge-Pea

other names: Wild Senna
height: 1 to 4 feet
season: July to October

The bright yellow flowers grow up and down the stem of this plant. While the flowers don't look like members of the pea family, the seed capsules do. The hairy pod may remind you of garden peas, but the seeds are small and hard.

Butterflyweed

other names: Orange Milkweed, Pleurisy Root, Chiggerweed
height: 12 to 30 inches
season: June to September

Butterflies love the nectar in these clustered, bright orange blossoms. Look closely at these unusual flowers. The petals are reflexed back, but other flower parts are erect. Early settlers chewed the roots to treat lung problems and used the fluffy seeds to stuff pillows. Some people decorated their hats with the feathery seeds.

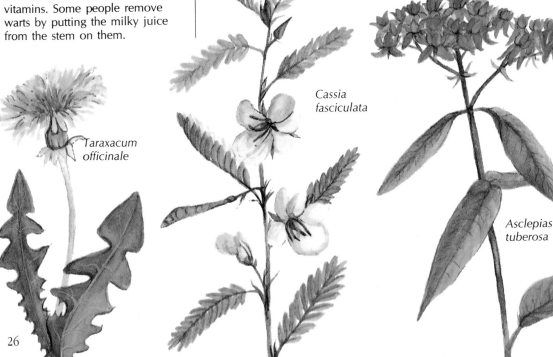

Taraxacum officinale

Cassia fasciculata

Asclepias tuberosa

Chicory

other names: Ragged Sailors
height: 1 to 4 feet
season: June to October

The roadsides of the mountains and foothills are lined with the light blue flowers of this plant. Each blossom lasts just one day. But chicory puts out a few new flowers each day, so there seem to be lots of blossoms. Some people think the tattered ends of the petals look like raggedy sailors dressed in blue. The young, green leaves make a tasty salad in early spring. Roasted chicory roots can be ground into powder and used to make a drink much like coffee.

Cichorium intybus

Ox-Eye Daisy

other names: Daisy
height: 1 to 2 feet
season: May to first frost

English people called this a "day's eye" because the flower opens each day and closes at night. The outer white rays surround a yellow center. Look through a magnifying glass for a closeup of the hundreds of tiny, yellow, tubular florets packed into the center.

Chrysanthemum leucanthemum

Black-Eyed Susan

other names: Brown-Eyed Susan
height: 1 to 3 feet
season: June to October

The bright yellow-orange rays attract insects, which find nectar in the drab, brown center disc of florets. This plant must prefer flying insects, because tiny barbs on its stem discourage crawling bugs. Livestock don't like to eat this plant, so when you see lots of these flowers in a pasture, it's overgrazed.

Rudbeckia hirta

Conclusion

"Over here! Look at me!" shout the bright colors of a wildflower. The showy blossom attracts us, but more importantly, it attracts insects and other flying and crawling visitors that pollinate it. Bees, moths, beetles, butterflies, hummingbirds, and even ants and bats are essential for wildflowers to make seeds.

So when you bend down to enjoy the sweet smell of a fresh blossom, remember to share the space with other creatures. Wildflowers may like us to look at them, but they depend on their other visitors for survival.

Glossary

Alternate	Not opposite each other
Annual	A plant that lives for one season
Anther	The part of the stamen containing pollen
Berry	A fleshy fruit containing seeds
Biennial	A plant that lives for two years
Bract	Leaflike scales
Bulb	A plant bud usually below the ground
Corm	A bulblike underground swelling of a stem
Composite	Flower heads composed of clusters of ray and disk flowers
Disk flower	Tubular florets in the center part of a composite flower head
Evergreen	Bearing green leaves or needles throughout the year
Filament	The stalk of the stamen
Floret	A small flower that is part of a cluster
Flower	Part of a plant containing male and/or female reproductive parts
Flower head	A dense cluster of flowers atop a stem
Fruit	A seed-bearing part of a plant
Habitat	The community where a plant naturally grows
Head	A dense cluster of flowers atop a stem
Herb	A seed plant with no woody tissue, whose stems die back to the ground each year
Irregular	Nonsymmetrical in shape
Nectar	Sweet liquid produced by flowers to attract insects
Opposite	Pairs of leaves opposite each other on a stem
Ovary	The part of the pistil that contains the developing seeds
Parasitic	Growing on and deriving nourishment from another plant
Pathfinders	Lines that guide insects to the nectar
Pedicel	The supporting stem of a single flower
Perennial	A plant that lives from year to year

Petals	Floral leaves inside the sepals that attract pollinators
Petiole	The stem supporting a leaf
Pistil	The seed-bearing organ of a flower
Pollen	Powderlike cells produced by the stamens
Ray flower	The flowers around the edge of a flower head; each flower may resemble a single petal
Reflexed	Bent or curved backward or downward
Regular	Alike in size and shape
Rhizome	Underground stem or rootstock
Saprophyte	A plant that lives on dead organic matter
Seed	Developed female egg
Seedpod	Sack enclosing the developed female egg(s)
Sepal	The outermost floral leaf that protects the delicate petals
Shrub	Low woody plant, usually having several stems
Spadix	Fleshy spike that bears flowers
Spathe	Leafy covering connected to the base of a spadix
Spur	Hollow appendage of a petal or sepal
Stamen	Pollen-producing organ of a flower
Stigma	The end of the pistil that collects pollen
Style	The slender stalk of a pistil
Succulent	A plant with thick, fleshy leaves or stems that conserve moisture
Tendril	Slender, twining extension of a leaf or stem
Tuber	A thickened underground stem having numerous buds
Whorl	Three or more leaves or branches growing from a common point

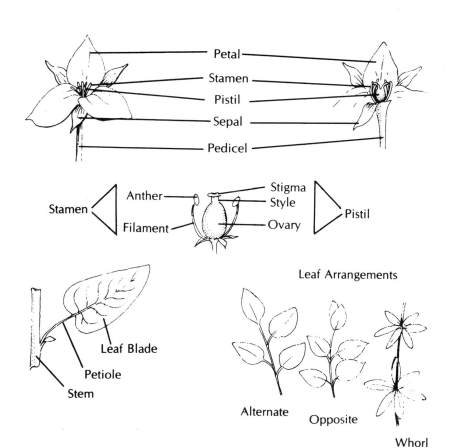

Where to See Wildflowers in North Carolina

There are many places to see wildflowers in North Carolina, including national parks, national forests, state parks, botanical gardens, and private parks. These reflect the rich botanical diversity of the state.

These state parks are especially good places to view wildflowers:

Seminole Canyon, Great Smoky Mountains National Park, 107 Park Headquarters Road Gatlinburg, TN 37738, (615) 436-1200
Almost any trail will have a great display of mountain wildflowers.

Blue Ridge Parkway, 200 BB&T Building, Asheville, NC 28801, (704) 259-0779
There are many great trails along this scenic roadway. Some of the best include the Tanawha Trail, Flat Rock, Linville Gorge, Crabtree Falls, Craggy Gardens, Mount Pisgah, and Richland Balsam.

Cape Hatteras National Seashore, Route 1, Box 675, Manteo, NC 27954, (919) 473-2113
This seashore offers many places to see beach vegetation, especially at Cape Hatteras itself.

North Carolina National Forests, P.O. Box 2750, Asheville, NC 28802, (704) 257-4200
There are four national forests in North Carolina. Two are in the mountains, one is in the Piedmont, and one is on the coast. Good mountain wildflower locations are Roan Mountain, Linville Gorge, the Pink Beds, Joyce Kilmer, and Standing Indians.

North Carolina State Parks, P.O. Box 27687, Raleigh, NC 27611-7687, (919) 733-7275
Several state parks have wonderful wildflower displays. These include Mount Mitchell in the mountains; Hanging Rock, Eno River, Olmstead, and Raven Rock in the Piedmont; and Merchant's Millpond and Hammock's Beach on the coast.

The Nature Conservancy, North Carolina Chapter, Carr Mill, Suite D12, Carrboro, NC 27510, (919) 967-7007
Many Nature Conservancy preserves are spectacular places to see wildflowers. Several worth visiting are Nags Head Woods on the coast and Bluff Mountain and Big Yellow in the mountains. Visitors are only allowed at the preserves as part of organized field trips.

North Carolina Botanical Garden, Box 3375 Totten Center, University of North Carolina, Chapel Hill, NC 27599, (919) 962-0522
This wonderful garden is full of native plants, organized by regions of the state. The garden also has several outlying preserves, including Penny's Bend north of Durham.

North Carolina Arboretum, P.O. Box 6617 Asheville, NC 28816, (704) 665-2492
This new garden under development near Asheville will become one of the premier gardens in the nation.

Grandfather Mountain, P.O. Box 732, Linville, NC 28646, (704) 733-4337
The privately owned mountain is crossed by wonderful trails. A fee is charged for hiking.